Exploring

G000070653

Exploring Shadeism

Find out more about the author and upcoming books online at https://www.sharonhh.com

Table of Contents

Foreword

EXPLORING SHADEISM was originally written as an MA research project. But, 20 years later, it's clear that the issues raised here are still important and still affect the everyday lives of people of colour.

With #blacklivesmatter, race, diversity and discrimination currently on the cultural agenda, it seems a good time to add this research to the conversation.

This is released pretty much as originally written. I hope you'll find it useful.

Sharon Hurley Hall

Introduction

In Western metropolitan centres where black people are a minority within the population, they are often seen as one undifferentiated mass, and indeed as Paul Gilroy has pointed out, often see themselves as such. He asserts that "British racism has generated turbulent economic, ideological, and political forces that have seemed to act upon the people they oppressed by concentrating their cultural identities into a single powerful configuration." [Gilroy, 1987: p.86] In other words, in the face of white racism, black people of varying hues and national background have banded together to take on a single 'black' identity. The fact that in London second and third generation Black Britons of all origins affect a Jamaican accent is a striking example of this. Indeed, the term 'black' has become a political designation that includes minority groups of different ethnicities.

Looking from the outside and judging from Western representations on TV advertisements and in other media, the Caribbean is also seen as a homogenous mass – a tropical paradise peopled by smiling natives unified in their desire to give tourists the holiday of a lifetime. But the reality could not be further from the truth.

Historically, a divide and rule policy was used to keep the inhabitants of the different islands from forging close links and thus being inclined to foment revolution. The legacy of that can still be seen today in the string of failed attempts at unity that have been part of the Caribbean scene since independence in the 1960s to 1980s. Caribbean nation states generally cling steadfastly to their national identities in defiance of economic logic and, as in the EU, opting out of legislation to which they have agreed in principle is a time-honoured practice.

The divisions inherited from the days of slavery also remain within individual communities. In multi-ethnic societies such as those in Trinidad or Guyana, division is made along the more 'traditional' lines of ethnicity; in other, less diverse societies (Barbados is a good example), discrimination is made on the basis of subtle differences in skin shade. This is the phenomenon which I have termed shadeism [Hurley, 1997].

Perhaps it is useful to explain at this point how it is that distinctions of shade have come about. After all, to the untrained eye, Caribbean inhabitants are all black. In slave societies, one of the perks of plantation ownership was the availability of a ready-made harem – slave women. When, as was inevitable, these women had children, the master had done himself the dual service of having had sexual relief and increased his slave population (a factor which no doubt became even more important when the slave trade was abolished early in the 18th century.) These slaves would have been of varying hues, with varying degrees of European features.

F. W. Knight offers a good description of the division of plantation society:

"The caste system represented the most notable aspect of the plantation society. The typical slave society had three legally defined castes stubbornly supported partly by force, partly by custom, and partly by impromptu legal ingenuity. In ascending order of social status (and often population size), these three castes were the slaves, the free persons of color, and the white persons. Each component required a separate set of criteria to define and distinguish it..." [Knight, 1990: p.122]

Given the fact that whiteness was a prized social asset, it is not surprising that this became a system for classifying and identifying people, and placing them within the social structure. It is generally felt that in many cases these light coloured slaves received preferential treatment, either in terms of getting easier jobs (not working in the fields), or being freed on the master's death.

"Slaves of mixed ancestry were not generally regarded as good field workers. As a result, there was a concentration of these slaves in urban areas and in the domestic, skilled and artisanal trades. These occupations provided both the exposure and the income that facilitated the movement from slavery to freedom, therefore reinforcing the notion that lightness of skin color lubricated social mobility, Consequently, slaves of mixed heritage felt that they were generally superior in rank to African and Afro-American slaves, and this sentiment permeated every society where the norms for grace and beauty were those established by the superordinate white sector." [Knight, 1990: p.128]

This stratification also existed among freed slaves:

"Within the intermediate stratum of the free persons of color, race and color – or more precisely complexion and shades of color – determined status and rank. In most cases, free mulattoes were considered (and considered themselves) to be superior in status to free blacks [Knight, 1990: p.123.]

This, then, is the framework within which shadeism exists.

As I will show, the peculiarities of Barbados' history (compared with that of its Caribbean neighbours) make it an ideal site for the study of shadeism. However, I will begin this paper by describing the phenomenon in more detail and examining it within the context of the wider Caribbean, focusing particularly on Caribbean history and literature.

I will then examine two theories that are useful in explaining why shade discrimination has taken root in the Caribbean. Both Frantz Fanon and Harry Hoetink site the origin firmly in slavery and deal, respectively, with its psychological and sociological impact on post-slave societies. As I will show, shadeism is a direct result of slavery – and the psychological and sociological impacts are still visible in the Caribbean today.

After a discussion of the research methods I have chosen, consisting of questionnaires, interviews and internet newsgroup postings, I will present my findings to attempt to find out whether, as I believe, the phenomenon still exists, and if it does, how it manifests itself. It will then be possible to draw some conclusions about shadeism and to consider how the subject could be studied further.

1. Context

One could argue that the experience of slavery is the bedrock on which Caribbean society has been founded. The expansion of sugar production in the mid to late seventeenth century, and the need for cheap labour to run the industry led to a booming slave trade. Eric Williams [1970: pp.177ff] describes how, across the Caribbean, different European colonisers came up with laws to regulate every aspect of the lives of the non-white residents. Slaves tended to come from different parts of Africa, were deliberately separated from others who spoke their language, and were forced to adopt the colonists' language (and with it their system of beliefs) wholesale. As Barbadian historian Hilary Beckles points out:

"The social culture of the Africans was degraded by the white community, and blacks were penalised for adhering too closely to it. Blacks responded in two ways to this intense social pressure. First, by taking underground those elements of culture which could survive without public display ... Second, by openly assimilating European-derived elements of the creole culture so as to achieve social and material betterment. [Beckles, 1990: p.52]

It is this latter response which is of particular relevance for this study.

David Lowenthal's 1972 study, *West Indian Societies* outlines the importance of race and colour in the West Indian context and explores both the resulting social structure and the history that has contributed to it. For example, he notes the stratification of people according to the amount of white blood they had [Lowenthal, 1972: p.95] and the importance of having 'good hair' (i.e. as near to European as possible). Lowenthal links this phenomenon to the distinctions made under slavery [Lowenthal, 1972: p.71] and points out throughout the book that many black people appear to be striving towards a European ideal.

By and large, however Caribbean history books make little explicit mention of shadeism; indeed, it is often only a small part of a wider exploration of regional history or society. One can only speculate about the reasons for this. Until relatively recently Caribbean history books were written outside the region, and perhaps discomfort over the legacy of slavery or even the insignificance (perhaps even invisibility) of the issue to people outside the region may have meant that it was not dealt with.

In Barbados, white Barbadians, who would almost certainly have had a different perspective on the issue, wrote some of the early history books. Certainly, although all the history books touch on social stratification during the time of slavery, until recently there was an almost universal silence about shade discrimination *per se*. Perhaps this stems from an unwillingness to name the phenomenon and thus give it power; perhaps it is a feeling that Caribbean people should get past that; or perhaps it is simply that it is so all-pervasive and so hard to quantify that no-one has dealt with it. It may be worth bearing in mind that many of the region's leading historians would have come to prominence either during the independence movements of the 1950s-1960s, or during the black power era of the 1970s, and their silence could simply reflect the public mood of unity during those periods. Where social stratification is mentioned, it is only within the context of a social regime imposed by the colonial masters. To my knowledge, nothing explores the phenomenon today, over 160 years after the end of slavery.

An examination of Caribbean literature, however, proves more fruitful. While it would be a mistake to assume that everything which appears in a novel is 'true', one can perhaps glean an inkling of the preoccupations of the people concerned, as Lukacs has stated elsewhere.

In *Passion and Exile: Essays in Caribbean Literature*, Frank Birbalsingh looks at how the novels of John Hearne deal with race and colour consciousness in Jamaica. Two statements are particularly noteworthy:

"Slavery was abolished in the 1830's but by means of a system of values social and economic apartheid based on skin colour, the European ex-masters were able to maintain dominance in Jamaican affairs until towards the end of the colonial era." [Birbalsingh, 1988: p.39]

and

"The basis of apartheid, race and colour consciousness, comprises a pernicious system of values which are universally accepted by blacks, browns and whites alike, and which declare in practice that white is equivalent to rich, black to poor, and intermediate shades of skin colour to corresponding rungs on upright, twin ladders of economic opportunity and social acceptance." [Birbalsingh, 1988: p.39]

Birbalsingh makes the link between colour and social and economic status which is vital to an understanding of shadeism. The Kaywana novels of Edgar Mittelholzer (of Guyana) also reveal this consciousness of shades and, further, show that different characteristics are attributed to people of different hues.

In *The Groundings with My Brothers*, Walter Rodney highlights another aspect of the phenomenon. This relates to the other features, apart from the shade of skin, which help to determine a person's acceptability, and supports Lowenthal's findings above:

"The language which is used by black people in describing ourselves shows how we despise our African appearance. 'Good hair' means European hair, 'good nose' means a straight nose, 'good complexion' means a light complexion. Everybody recognises how incongruous and ridiculous such terms are, but we continue to use them and to express our support of the assumption that white Europeans have the monopoly of beauty, and that black is the incarnation of ugliness." [Rodney, 1969: pp.32-33]

The quotation from Rodney also points to some ambivalence about skin colour on the part of black people, for while we admit that it's wrong, we still do it. It seems that Caribbean people are doomed to repeat endlessly the patterns of slave society. The case of Haiti, to which I will refer again later, tragically illustrates this. One possible explanation is that whiteness remains as potent a symbol of power and freedom as it was during the days of slavery. After all, in Barbados and many other Caribbean nations, most of the economic power is held by the white descendants of plantation owners – the fact that political power is in the hands of blacks is relatively unimportant in that context. With few exceptions, to be white in the Caribbean is to have money, power, and the freedom to do anything or nothing – it is, in many cases, to occupy the top rung of society.

Black literature, both inside and outside the Caribbean, provides striking evidence of preoccupation with skin shade and European features. For example, Toni Morrison's *The Bluest Eye* tells of a dark-skinned little girl who wanted to be white because of her perception that this was where true social acceptability lay. And many Caribbean women will recognise themselves in the little girl described by bell hooks:

"Her skin is dark. Her hair chemically straightened. Not only is she fundamentally convinced that straightened hair is more beautiful than curly, kinky, natural hair, she believes that lighter skin makes one more worthy, more valuable in the eyes of others." [hooks, 1992: p.3]

It is noteworthy that the two authors I have cited have emerged from a society which itself has a history of the enslavement of black people.

Having looked at the wider Caribbean context, I now wish to turn to Barbados. There are several reasons for my choice of this area as a field for study. It is commonly felt that because of the particular history of the island, social stratification by shade is both more visible and endemic than in other Caribbean regions. From the days of slavery and until well into the 20th century, Barbados was made up primarily of two populations: white Europeans of British descent, and black African slaves. Other islands experienced greater diversity, both in the ethnic mix of their colonisers and in that of their slaves and indentured labourers. Another factor is the geography of the island. With no mountains in which to hide, escapes were less likely to be successful, so that the Barbadian slave population was, both literally and metaphorically, a captive one.

Two examples tend to suggest that there is some truth in this observation. In *The Changing Face of the Caribbean* Irene Hawkins comments that "Many observers maintain that the stratification of Barbadian society according to subtle degrees of skin colour is one of the most rigid in the area." [Hawkins, 1976: p.70], but she does not explore the phenomenon in detail. Meanwhile, a folk poem by Andrea Gollop of Barbados describes the phenomenon:

"You evah stop to study

Hummuch shades Buhbajans got?

Rangin' from black to backra -

Startin' wid "black-as-de-pot …

B'looka life - wid all dem shades,

Bajans en know no hate!

We en ha' nuh time fuh prejudice -

We does only discriminate!"

[Gollop, date unknown]

2. Theoretical base

In searching for a way to explain and attempt to understand shadeism, there was not much material to draw on. However, Harry Hoetink's 1967 study of Caribbean race relations does deal in some measure with the segmentation of Caribbean society in the various forms in which it appears. Although Hoetink does not deal explicitly with Barbados, he states that:

> "... in all Caribbean societies, a number of similarities developed – in socio-economic structure, racial segmentation, social institutions and cultural and social values, traditions and stereotypes – which justify us in viewing the Caribbean as a geographically defined social entity." [Hoetink, 1967: p.2]

and while I would argue against seeing the Caribbean as one entity, there is nonetheless some merit in his argument.

2.1 The somatic norm – Harry Hoetink

In *Caribbean Race Relations: A Study of Two Variants* [1967] Harry Hoetink compares two models of Caribbean society during and after slavery: the societies created by the Iberian colonists and the North-West Europeans respectively. One of the principal differences lies in the attitude towards Negro blood. Drawing on a number of sources Hoetink illustrates that in Spanish/Portuguese culture, this was not regarded as tainted. The history of domination by the Moors meant that darker skins were less strange (I would argue, however, that this same phenomenon is partly responsible for the prejudices which affect non-whites today). He also gives religious reasons, describing Catholicism as unifying where Protestantism emphasised the individual and was thus divisive.

But Hoetink does not accept these explanations unreservedly. Rather, he goes deeper to examine the concept of race relations. He divides these into two categories: the non-intimate relations between the races in superficial, everyday intercourse [Hoetink, 1967: p.21] and the willingness of members of the different races to enter into intimate personal relations based on social equality, particularly characterised by the willingness to enter into sexual relations [Hoetink, 1967: p.22]. While the first category has no influence on social stratification, the second "determines the structural dynamism of mixed societies". [Hoetink, 1967: p.23]

According to Hoetink the area of race relations has not been adequately examined in investigations of the differences between the Iberian and north European model. He claims that social reality forces a distinction between at least three categories of non-whites: the slave, the Negro and the mulatto or coloured [Hoetink, 1967: p.23]. He briefly outlines some of the provisions of the various codes governing colonial society during the time of slavery, but goes on to point out that "Slavery was not exclusively or principally an indication of the cruelty, or liberality, of race relations, but above all an economic institution [Hoetink, 1967: pp.25-26]. He therefore concludes that conditions of slavery had very little to do with superficial differences between the two models.

Hoetink then examines Caribbean societies, starting with the Iberian model (in, for example, Cuba and Brazil) where the physical ideal and upper social stratum is mainly white; the lowest stratum is mostly black; and the middle one is mixed. The situation is similar in the north-west European variant, but with less flexibility within the groups. He then looks at the situation in the British Caribbean, as it then was, and states that "Being white has always put a person at the top of the social ladder in this society, while a black skin has placed him automatically on the lower rung" [Hoetink, 1967: p.43].

In speaking of Trinidad he says:

"There is a variety of 'shade' discrimination in the coloured intermediate group in Trinidad, 'shade' implying not exclusively colour of the skin but also other typically Negroid features. The closer the approximation to European features, the more likely is the individual man both to get acceptance as an individual and to achieve mobility by marrying someone even closer to the European in skin colour, hair and facial characteristics" [Hoetink, 1967: p.44].

The same could have been said of many Caribbean societies.

Hoetink concludes that it is rare for intimate social relations between the races to take place in Caribbean societies. He then examines the concept of the plural society, in which the various segments mix but do not combine [Hoetink, 1967: p.90 ff.] While Hoetink does not believe it holds true for current analysis of these societies, nonetheless it is a useful starting point, he says.

Hoetink then goes on to examine some of the characteristics of a segmented society which he defines as:

"a society which *at its moment of origin* consists of at least two groups of people of different races and culture, each having its own social institutions and social structure; each of these groups ... having its own rank in the social structure; and society as a whole being governed by one of the segments." [Hoetink, 1967: p. 96]

This picture is true of most of the former slave societies of the Caribbean.

Hoetink claims that 'race' underpins this segmentation [Hoetink, 1967: p.98 ff.] He outlines three types of segmented societies: one in which there is no mobility between the segments (as in the U.S.); one in which there is limited mobility (the British Caribbean) ; and one in which the maximum social rise is possible (Brazil is an example) [Hoetink, 1967: p.101]. It is the second of these that principally concerns me. In this, as in the first type, mixing is inhibited by playing the race card. Hoetink also examines the case of Haiti as an example of what would happen if the dominant segment were to be removed. What did happen is that the next in rank, i.e. the mulattos stepped in. As he explains:

"If ... physical characteristics continue to be the determinants of social rank, the elimination of the originally dominant segment will not have resulted in homogeneity, but in an initial structural simplification of the segmentation." [Hoetink, 1967: p.109]

Hoetink here argues for a drift towards homogenisation as the inevitable consequence, but events and other critics on whom I shall elaborate later have shown that this is not the case.

Hoetink then introduces the concept of the 'somatic norm image', [Hoetink, 1967: p.120] rejecting the term 'race' as loaded with racist, biological and physiological notions which do not cover socially communicable phenomena. He defines it as:

> "the complex of physical (somatic) characteristics which are accepted by a group as its norm and ideal. Norm, because it is used to measure aesthetic appreciation; ideal, because usually no individual ever in fact embodies the somatic norm image of his group" [Hoetink, 1967: p.120].

This, he says, is a socio-psychological concept. He explains that if two races acknowledge that man is made in God's image their concept of god will still differ in line with their own appearance, so if race a has green skin, that will be their somatic norm image [Hoetink, 1967: p.121]. In the Orient, for example the images of beauty that are upheld are those that are naturally found among Orientals: pale skin, long hair, etc. Images of the Christ figure often look Oriental. Compare this with the millions of black people worldwide worshipping a distinctly European Christ figure, who is invariably blond and blue-eyed.

Hoetink acknowledges that his concept may meet with some resistance and points out that refusal to acknowledge the existence of a somatic norm in fact validates it, as it underlines the awareness of the dominant position:

"Sociologically the attitudes which two very different groups adopt towards one another within one society is an expression of their power-relationship and of their subjective insight into the extent to which the position of one is threatened by the other." [Hoetink, 1967: p.129]

He explains that in a society where one segment is dominant both numerically and socially, the second group will be seen as exotic and socially tolerated. This could also be seen as a metaphor for the West versus the Rest discourse. However, in a truly segmented society, and in particular where a minority dominates a majority, the reverse is true. Through a process of one-way transmission, the somatic norm of the dominant segment also becomes that of the subordinate segment. Hoetink adds that even when the dominant segment is removed, as in the case of Haiti cited above, the somatic norm remains the same, as long as that segment's right to a dominant position continues to hold sway [Hoetink, 1967: p.135].

Hoetink does not deal with the psychological effects of this phenomenon. For that we must turn to Fanon, as I shall do later.

He then redefines a segmented society as one

"in which two or more groups occur which had originally, apart from their cultural differences, clearly different somatic norm images, of which that of the dominant segment has, in the process of intersegmentary acculturation, been adopted and accepted by the lower segment or segments." [Hoetink, 1967: p.137]

I believe that this provides a convincing explanation of shadeism, for there is no doubt that it is the white, European image that is the somatic norm of many Caribbean societies. Adoption of this norm, Hoetink states, results in the "tendency in the lower segments to mingle with the dominant segment in order to spare progeny from the sense of non-fulfilment of its somatic norm image. [Hoetink, 1967: p.151-2]

Hoetink then highlights somatic distance, the difference between one's original somatic norm and that of the dominant segment. He outlines some of the terms to describe black people, and points out that their characteristics are almost universally regarded as ugly

[Hoetink, 1967: p.165]. Hoetink concludes that the presence of a whiter somatic norm in the Caribbean will impede any move towards racial homogenisation, and his re-examination of the situation in a 1985 paper on 'Race and Colour in the Caribbean' bears out this view:

"So far, mutual suspicion, negative stereotyping, and a sense of identity nurtured by what is distinctive in each group rather than what they have in common have proved hard to overcome" [Hoetink, quoted in Oostindie, 1996: p7]

2.2 Internalising racism – Frantz Fanon

Where Hoetink looks at sociological explanations for the segmentation of black society, giving reasons that have more to do with power relations than anything else, Frantz Fanon takes a different tack. As a West Indian, Frantz Fanon is himself heavily implicated in questions of colonial society, race relations and shadeism. But Fanon's relevance is in his own speciality of psychology. It is his work on how slavery and colonial society have affected the black man, seen principally in *Black Skin, White Masks*, that I propose to examine.

Fanon's principal argument is that black people (or, to use his terminology, the black man) have internalised racism to the point where whiteness is the epitome of any achievement. Early in the book he makes the striking statement: "For the black man there is only one destiny. And it is white." [Fanon, 1986: p.12]. He goes on to say that: "The colonized is elevated above his jungle status in proportion to his adoption of the mother country's cultural standards. He becomes whiter as he renounces his blackness, his jungle" [Fanon, 1986: p.18] He makes a similar point further on [Fanon, 1986: p.98]. Fanon is suggesting here that colonised black people have internalised the inferiority conferred upon them since the days of slavery by Europeans. This seems to reinforce Hoetink's point that where one group is dominant in a segmented society, that group's norms will become the ideal for that society, for, as he states: "not only must the black man be black; he must be black in relation to the white man." [Fanon, 1986: p.110]

But Fanon probes more deeply than Hoetink into what is going on in the unconscious of both coloniser and colonised. He speaks of the European's need to feel superior – this is why he creates an inferior in the black man [Fanon, 1986: p.93]. The marking of this difference is fundamental to white identity, as David Theo Goldberg succinctly puts it:

"Seemingly in control of the terms of racial definition, whites necessarily depend for their racial power on being recognised as white by the Other defined in racial terms precisely as black. Thus whites require recognition *qua* white by those whose very human existence they deny" [Goldberg, D T in Gordon et al (Ed) 1996: p.182]

In other words, the fostering of the notion that white was superior through law, writings, education and other discourses helped to reinforce this idea both among blacks and whites, thus validating colonialism and white superiority in a never-ending cycle.

Although Fanon does not deal explicitly with the question of shade, he illustrates the effects of racism (from which shadeism emanates) on the black psyche. He speaks of how the black man is regarded by the white man as less than human, given to base characteristics. And when a black man is raised in a white dominated colonial system, he must also see black people as such, for it is not until he leaves his island that he is aware that he too is black. This produces a kind of psychic confusion, a mental tension between what he feels himself to be and what he recognises that he is. It is not difficult to see how this could produce a reverence of and striving for whiteness, which although it may at times be unconscious, is a powerful motive force.

Again, I believe Fanon outlines the psychological confusion that lies at the heart of shadeism, or, as Homi Bhabha puts it in his foreword to the 1986 edition of *Black Skin, White Masks:*

"the experience of dispossession and dislocation – psychic and social – which speaks to the condition of the marginalized, the alienated, those who have to live under the surveillance of a sign of identity and fantasy that denies their difference." [Fanon, 1986: p. xxiv]

2.3 How Hoetink's and Fanon's theories explain shadeism

To sum up, Hoetink argues that where one group is dominant in society, that group's somatic norm (its ideal of beauty and social acceptability) will become that of society as a whole. This is what happened in colonial slave societies. In what he refers to as the north-west European variant, the somatic norm was whiter than the Iberian variant for historical reasons. Fanon says the same thing, but takes a psychological approach. Thus, the experience of slavery had both psychological and sociological effects. Sociologically, it produced a multi-coloured society in which everyone was trying desperately to avoid being at the bottom – the bottom being black. Psychologically, it produced a reverence for all things white – it is interesting to note that even today there is an ambivalent attitude to technology or education brought back from the West. If it is brought by a white man, it is readily accepted; if, however, the bearer is a black man, he will find it harder to be heard. It seems to me that these two theories adequately explain why shadeism exists today, and why it is likely to for some time.

3. Research methods

This research topic posed a number of methodological problems. As little has been published on the subject, and demographic surveys of Barbados do not recognise skin shade, I undertook some empirical research into shadeism in Barbadian society. I have previously explained my reasons for choosing this country as a field of study.

In some respects, I was in the advantageous position mentioned by Van Dijk (1987) of being both an insider and an outsider at the same time, as I lived in Barbados for 14 years and have now lived outside the country for seven years. This meant that I was aware of the phenomenon and some of the ways in which it was manifested. However, I have had to be reflexive about my own position as a dark-skinned black woman who has experienced some of the prejudices that go with shade discrimination. I have also had to be rigorous about not allowing my preconceptions to influence my research, though it would be difficult to achieve a completely neutral position.

The bulk of my research was collected via a questionnaire. I thought that given my own shade, some people might hesitate to reveal their true feelings, so the questionnaires were handed out and collected by intermediaries. The questionnaire seeks background data about the nationality, ethnic origin, level of education and skin shade of the respondents. It attempts to discover whether they think shadeism exists, whether they have been affected by it, how it has affected their choice of partners or friends, and whether they would choose to be lighter or darker. A detailed analysis is given below.

Most of the questions were multiple choice to allow for some similarity in terms of analysis, but there were also some free choice responses. Unfortunately, some people refused to answer the more pertinent questions.

The questionnaire was backed up by interviews of some of the respondents. Not many people consented to be interviewed so the results cannot claim to be conclusive, but responses do provide a guide to the thinking of some people in their late 20s-mid 30s. I also conducted one interview via email.

In addition I tried to gain information from the Internet via newsgroup postings on the subject. This had some response and I was able to get some general feedback by this method, and to do some follow-up interviews.

While none of these methods can claim to be exhaustive, the three together help to build up a general picture of how shadeism is understood, perceived and experienced by Barbadians of all ages, economic levels and skin shades.

4. Questionnaire analysis

A total of 103 people responded to the questionnaires; however two questionnaires were discarded because of insufficient information. The analysis is therefore based on 101 responses. Of these, 68 were female and 33 male. I intend to present the overall findings, followed by a separate analysis for males and females to attempt to determine to what extent gender may have affected the results. Not all questions were answered by all respondents, and unless it is germane to the analysis I have not indicated these non-answers. All percentages given are approximate, and the actual number of respondents is shown in brackets.

4.1 Overall analysis

Most of the respondents were in the 22-30 (32), 31-40 (25) and 41-55 (24) age groups. Only three respondents were non-Barbadian, and most respondents had been born in Barbados. Some 83% described themselves as of Black Caribbean origin; nearly 7% described themselves as Black Other, and nearly 8% as mixed race/biracial. Fifty-five percent (56) respondents were single and 40.5% (41) married. Over 30% of all respondents had a first degree and 26% had experienced further education. This is not surprising in the Barbadian context, where a high premium is placed on education, which is free up to tertiary level. Most of the respondents were medium (38) or dark skinned (44).

Fifty-eight percent of respondents said they were not aware of any discrimination shown to them because of skin shade, while nearly 32% said that they were. However, nearly 82% of respondents said they believed shade discrimination was common. Although this appears contradictory, it merely indicates that while most people believe in the existence of shadeism, not many of them have been personally affected by it. This is borne out by the answers to Question 14, where some 45% of respondents believed shade discrimination happened occasionally, about 31% believed it happened frequently and nearly 4% believed it happened infrequently. Only 4 people believed it never happened.

I then attempted to assess whether skin shade affected respondents' choice of partner. This question posed some problems. I asked respondents to describe their partner's shade, and those who did not have a partner to describe their ideal partner's shade. In retrospect, the latter question would have been adequate for my purposes. As it was, some people answered both questions, and some neither. In this section, therefore, I shall present figures rather than percentages to avoid distorting the overall analysis.

Most people said there was no significant difference between their shade and that of their partner (29) or ideal partner (23). Nineteen people had a significantly darker partner, 13 a significantly lighter partner, and 8 said they'd never thought about it. Only one person said their ideal partner would be significantly darker, 3 said significantly lighter and 35 had never thought about it. Some 83% of respondents said shade had not or would not influence their choice. Interestingly, four people – three women and one man – said it would. I will expand on this in the following section.

Over 90 percent said shade would not influence their choice of friends, but some 6% (6) – all of them women – said it would. Some possible explanations for this are suggested in the following section.

Most people said their romantic interests had come from a variety of ethnic backgrounds. Some 18% had dated exclusively dark-skinned people, some 11 per cent exclusively medium skinned people and some 7 percent exclusively light skinned people. Less than 3 percent had dated a different ethnic group exclusively. Again, this may reflect the Barbadian context, where inter-racial mixing is less common than in other Caribbean territories. Using Hoetink's theories, one could also surmise that there was less mixing between racial groups because of the sharp polarisation between dominant and subordinate segments.

Many products exist which are used for 'toning' (or lightening the skin). Products such as Ambi and Esoterica contain hydro-quinone (which in quantities over 2% can be extremely damaging to the skin). These products are used by many black women and make regular appearances in magazine advertising. People have been known to use them to lighten their skin, although in these days of political correctness not many people will admit to using it for this purpose. Most of the people polled (some 79%) had never used such creams. However, nearly 18% had.

Finally the hypothetical question about a life threatening situation in which only two remedies were available – one would make you two shades darker, the other two shades lighter - proved problematic. Some people were diverted by the medical aspect of the question, and commented on the need to avoid side effects of any kind; while others could not bring themselves to commit to either option.

Responses were fairly evenly split between those who chose to be darker (33%) and those who chose to be lighter (29%). This may reflect changing attitudes, or a move towards political correctness. Judging by the responses of the people who consented to be interviewed, some of whom changed their initial responses to this question, there is still considerable ambivalence on the question of skin shade. I sensed that respondents felt a tension between choosing the darker option, which political correctness requires them to validate, and the lighter one, which many thought would make life easier.

Respondents were also asked to rate the attractiveness of a number of celebrities of different skin shades. These were: Mariah Carey, Colin Jackson, Janet Jackson, Denzel Washington, Brandy, Wesley Snipes, Diana Ross, Halle Berry, Mario van Peebles, Angela Basset, Lenny Kravitz and Whitney Houston. Although I attempted to choose celebrities in different areas and of different skin shades, many respondents did not answer this question fully because they did not know who the people were. Among both men and women, Halle Berry came out as the most attractive woman, and Denzel Washington as the most attractive man. It is interesting to note that Halle Berry is much lighter in complexion than Denzel Washington, which lends some credence to the belief that darker skin is less of a disadvantage for men in terms of perceptions of sexual attractiveness, although it is impossible to be conclusive on the basis of this limited survey. There was no obvious correlation between the shade of the respondents and the way they rated the stars.

The survey also contained a question relating to hair type, as this is often perceived to be a variable in the question of shadeism. However, when I attempted to analyse the response, realised that I had not requested enough other information for a conclusive analysis and thus I discarded this question from the final analysis.

4.2 Comparative analysis of male and female responses

Of the 33 male respondents, 27% (9) were in the 22-30 age group, 24% (8) in the 31-40 age group, 36% (12) in the 41-55 age group and 6% (2) in the 56-65 age group. Two respondents did not give their ages. All of the respondents were Barbadian, and only one had been born outside Barbados. Some 42% (14) men were single, 54%

(18) married and one divorced. Over 80% (27) were of black Caribbean origin, and 18% (6) described themselves as black other, including: one man who described his origin as African/European/Indian (M16) and one who described his origin as black American (M15). There were four mixed race men, 3 black Caucasian (M1, M3, M31) and one black/Indian/Caucasian (M23).

Of the 68 female responses, over 33% (23) of women were aged 22-30, 25% (17) 31-40, 18% (12) 41-55, 14% (10) 16-21, 4% (3) 56-65 and 1% (one) over 66. Sixty-five women described themselves as Barbadian, 2 as other and one did not answer. 58 were born in Barbados, nine elsewhere and one did not answer. Of the 68 women, 62% (42) were single, 34% (23) married, 3% (2) divorced and one living with partner. Some 83% (57) described their ethnic origin as Black Caribbean, (3%) 2 as black American, 1% (1) as black other and 11% (8) as mixed race (black/Indian or black/white/Indian). There were two responses from people describing themselves as white/Caucasian.

The levels of education of the male respondents varied quite considerably. Three percent (1) had a school-leaving certificate, 18% (6) O-levels, 6% (2) A-levels, 30% (10) had been in further education, another 30% (10) had a first degree, 6% (2) had a masters and 6% (2) a doctorate. The levels of education of the female respondents were also quite varied. Some 31% (21) had a first degree, 24% (16) had been in further education, 18% (12) had O-levels, 7% (5) a school-leaving certificate and 4% (3) A-levels, 8% (6) a masters, and just under 3% (2) a doctorate.

Sixty-three percent (21) of men described themselves as dark-skinned, 27% (9) as medium-skinned, 6% (2) as light-skinned and 3% (1) as very light-skinned. Only one woman described herself as very dark-skinned. Just over 33% (23) said they were dark-skinned, 43% (29) as medium, 18% (12) as light skinned and nearly 5% (3) as very light-skinned. Some people said they had difficulty in describing their shade, and many chose medium as a safe option. These figures could reflect people's actual skin shade, but could also indicate that, particularly for women, describing themselves as dark-skinned carries negative connotations.

Asked whether they were aware of any discrimination because of their skin shade, 24% (8) of men said yes, 60% (20) said no. However 78% (26) said they believed shade discrimination was common and only 21% (7) that it wasn't. As I explained above, this is not as contradictory as it initially appeared, indicating that not many of the respondents had been on the receiving end of shade discrimination. Some 30% (10) said it was frequent, 48% (16) occasional and just 3% (1) infrequent.

Some 35% of women (24) said they had experienced discrimination or favouritism because of the shade of their skin, 57% (39) said they hadn't and 5 did not answer. However, more than 82% (56) believed shade discrimination was common, while only 12% (8) said it wasn't. Thirty-one percent of women (21) said it happened frequently, 44% (30) occasionally, and nearly 5% (3) infrequently.

The fact that a higher percentage of women than men appear to have experienced discrimination because of their skin shade (and to believe that it is common) lends some credence to the theory that women are more affected by the phenomenon than men. This may be because of the greater commodification of women in the socio-sexual marketplace. The responses were spread fairly evenly across all age groups, indicating that it is not simply a phenomenon that affects the older generations, as some believe.

Of the respondents who had experienced shadeism, some were able to give examples. The issues raised by the respondents include the effect of shade on job prospects, marriageability and perception of worth, and comments were received from males and females of various ages and backgrounds. I have grouped these below under the main themes which emerged.

Service

'When going to a popular bar I was told it was closed yet while leaving I saw the door being opened for people of lighter complexion whom I am sure were patrons' (M2)

'Preferential treatment of students of high/lighter complexion and service in stores' (M15)

'When shopping in stores sales clerks readily offer assistance to persons of lighter colour or white people.' (F22)

'When writing cheques I don't often have to show ID, but many black people do' (F26)

School

' At school teachers show more interest in students with lighter complexions' (F22)

'Teachers have favoured me despite behaviour.' (M33)

Romance/attractiveness

'Girlfriends have said they like my complexion.' (M33)

'Guys liking me simply because I was light-skinned.' (F1)

'Male preference towards me as opposed to another with a darker skin tone' (F36)

'I think people find me more attractive than they would if I were darker. However, many people have commented that my eyelashes are 'too curly'. I have been in beauty contests where the lightest-skinned contestant is slated to win, even though her features might be less pleasing than those of the darker skinned entrants' (F59)

'People are more willing to criticise your grooming if you are dark-skinned. My students often comment on the skin shade thing and I've been able to provide a positive role model to dark skinned students who have been victims of discrimination. Bajan men tend to go for the mixed 'Trinidad look' light skin long hair' (F11)

'By a family member who is lighter than I am and felt my hairstyle was too African' (F10)

'During childhood on occasion people seemed to compare me favourably with my sister who is slightly darker than I am.' (F70)

'In Barbados light-skinned people are often seen as more attractive' (F64)

Employment

'Various jobs had little potential because I did not fit' (M33)

'In one instance I got a job because the boss favoured light skinned people.' (F64)

Social

'Primary school – black girls hating me for having white friends'; age 10 – being put out of a white girl's house for no reason;' (F1)

Other

'people thinking that I feel that I am better or 'great' by looking at me' (F1)

Respondents were asked to describe the shade of their partner relative to their own. Single respondents were asked to describe the shade of their ideal partner. However, as explained above, some respondents answered both sections, so the total responses for this section do not tally.

Of the male respondents, 10 said their partner was significantly lighter, 1 significantly darker, 12 no significant difference, 2 never thought about it and 8 did not answer. Two said their ideal partner would be significantly lighter, 8 no significant difference, 12 never thought about it and 11 did not answer. Asked if shade would or had influenced their choice, 3% (1) said yes, over 84% (28) said no, and 6% (2)didn't know. Asked whether skin shade influenced their choice of friends, over 96% (32) said no and 1 didn't know. Asked to describe the shade of most of their partners, 6% (2) said light-skinned, 9% (3) said medium, 9% (3) said dark-skinned, 3% (1) said a different ethnic group and 63% (21) a variety.

Of the females respondents, 3 said their partner was significantly lighter, 18 significantly darker, 17 no significant difference, 6 never thought about it and 8 did not answer. One said their ideal partner would be significantly lighter, one significantly darker, 15 no significant difference, 23 never thought about it and 28 did not answer. Asked if shade would or had influenced their choice, just over 4% (3) said yes, over 80% (55) said no, and over 8% (6) didn't know. Asked whether skin shade influenced their choice of friends, over 86% (59) said no, some 9% (6) said yes and 2 didn't know. Asked to describe the shade of most of their partners, 7% (5) said light-skinned, 11% (8) said medium, nearly 24% (16) said dark-skinned, 3% (2) said a different ethnic group and 47% (32) a variety.

The figures show some similarity between the profile of males and females' partners, although it is interesting that more women than men said shade influenced their choice of partner, and their choice of friends. This may be because of social pressure to conform to an agreed standard. Also it is worth noting that in some girls schools, there is a sort of informal segregation during breaks based on ethnic and economic lines (*see Interview 3*), so friends could well be chosen for these reasons. I do not know what the position is in boys' schools.

Twelve percent of men (4) said they had used skin lightening creams, while 84% (28) said they hadn't. I found it surprising that so many men had used these products as they are generally perceived to be the preserve of women. One male used it to 'even' his skin tone, the rest for scars, sunburn or acne. Over 21% of women had used these products, while some 76% had not. Only one woman (F40) said she had used the cream to lighten her skin, the rest said they had used the cream for blemishes, 'evening' skin tone. As is pointed out in Interview 2 below, there are no advertisements for products to even skin to the darker shade – suggesting that a lighter shade is always more desirable and socially acceptable.

Respondents were presented with a choice of being two shades darker or two shades lighter. This proved a difficult question for many to answer, with one or two respondents describing the question as 'sick'. One even said 'we are all equal under God's eyes. Over 30% of men (9) chose to be lighter, while 27% (9) chose to be darker. Over 27% of women (19) chose to be lighter, while 35% (24) chose to be darker.

Reasons for choosing lighter ranged from being more photogenic (M17) to being more natural (M13, F28), while some people preferred to be darker because of skin cancer problems (F3), and a general feeling of being happy the way they were (F4). Some women who were light skinned didn't want to get any lighter. Comments included:

Lighter

'It's easier to regain your natural skin colour if lighter. Also I think a lighter skin colour would make me more attractive. It's also a more accepted skin colour' (M4)

'I am dark enough!' (M32)

'I am the darkest of a mixed couple's children and it would be less conspicuous to be lighter.' (F10)

'To be two shades darker I think that I would be pressured (mocked) by my peers and society as a whole because of the way in which they are socialised, and would be subjected to even greater discrimination. To avoid all the problems associated with very dark skin I would select medicine B' (F20)

'I would choose medicine B because I am already light-skinned and I like my colour. I don't know what being darker feels like' (F43)

'I find I am more attractive when my skin shade is lighter' (F44)

'Although I know it is silly, I would not want to have to deal with all the comments about how dark I've become. People act as if it is a sin to be darker, and it is easier not to have to go through that.' (F59) This resonates with Rodney's comments above [Rodney, 1969: pp.32-33].

Darker

'I am already dark skinned and therefore medicine A would be more comfortable for me. As I am happy with my dark skin it would be less drastic than B' (M9)

'I would be very pale and sickly looking if I were two shades lighter.' (F1)

'The blacker the berry the sweeter the juice.' (F53)

'I love being dark-skinned … it's not that I don't like the lighter skin tone, but I feel personally I'm more beautiful dark.' (F4)

Neither

'A lose/lose situation. I would be uncomfortable with either option … I have relatives and friends …from cream-complexioned to chocolate to burnt! I appreciate their

beauty but I don't know that I could make such a choice.'
(M16)'

'I really don't want to be any shade other than the one I am.'
(F11)

It is difficult to gauge to what extent the responses given indicate a change in the perception of dark skin. Rather, I think the questionnaires as a whole prove that people remain ambivalent about the issue, and as the interviews will show, the instinctive response may differ from the reasoned one.

The fact that so many more women than men commented on this issue suggests that it is more personal for them. In modern society, there is a lot of pressure on women to be all things to all men, to conform to a certain image – shadeism itself is another manifestation of that.

Respondents were also asked for their general comments on the issue of shadeism, and these were very revealing, suggesting that it is an issue that lies just beneath the surface of Barbadian life.

'Shade discrimination is common in Barbados but the situation is complicated by other factors such as perceived socio-economic group and status. It is difficult to identify whether shade discrimination in itself is only factor affecting somebody's actions.' (M3)

'Shadeism is practised but it's so hidden that you only notice it by how [people] look and speak to you. You notice it also in stores ... it is felt that people of colour can't spend, ... attendants give persons of lighter colour more attention and less attitude' (M4)

'If you look at TV ads in Barbados, the majority of actors are light skinned yet most Bajans are dark-skinned' (M9)

'Anybody who thinks that shadeism does not exist is not being honest.' (M13)

'There is obviously some evidence of shadeism. It is not talked about as openly as it should but it exists. Many people still have a preference for lighter skinned people. It is most evident in some areas of employment. It also determines things like promotion in some firms.' (M25)

'There is a greater chance of advancement if one has a lighter skin shade.' (M26)

'Hair type affects my choice of partner not skin colour' (M31)

'Shadeism does exist. It will never go away. Fairer is always better, or so the majority thinks.' (F7)

'People at makeup counters are often unwilling to serve or not trained to give advice to dark skinned customers. Black men have a problem with colour. They generally are looking for a lighter skinned woman with long hair.' (F11)

'In my early childhood I did consider light skinned people to be prettier. However, now I think that dark skin is just as attractive.' (F14)

'Discrimination on shade exists here in male/female unions in particular. Fairer skin is at a premium. The situation has however changed significantly relative to the past.' (F25)

'I went to a bank and on the first and second floors I saw one "black" black person. It can't be possible that only light skinned and brown skinned people were the only ones qualified for those positions.' (F39)

'I'm not prejudiced – whites do have a variety of friends, but obviously their preference is their own. Some blacks on the other hand have more respect for people who are light skinned or white and often fight hard for their friendship, and can't seem to realise slavery done. However you look at it most of us stick with our own kind, whatever that is.' (F43)

'It is a well-known fact that people with lighter skin appear more attractive than dark-skinned people. When I was at school in the 50s, the girls with fair skin got preferential treatment. They were the ones who got the jobs in the banks and department stores' (F51)

'In my opinion, shade discrimination is most noticeable in the romance department. Men like the 'browning' with the soft hair. And it is not only Caribbean men – you only have to look at the music videos out of the US – a lot of women are lighter complexioned.' (F66)

The comments above lead me to believe that shadeism is still prevalent and affects the lives of people today.

I made several attempts to see if any correlation existed between, for example, skin shade and occupation; skin shade and choice of partner; skin shade and awareness of shadeism, but found nothing conclusive. It appears that shadeism affects most people of different ages, shades and educational backgrounds. While it is experienced differently by everyone, many people appear to have some experience of it, whether positive or negative. The one correlation that I was able to make was between skin shade and marriageability. The findings led me to surmise that dark-skinned women were less marketable than lighter skinned women – a theory which is borne out by many of the respondents' comments.

5. Interviews

Only three of the people who completed questionnaires consented to be interviewed, and these were in the 22-30 and 31-40 age range. While they cannot by any means be taken as representative, they do give some idea as to the possible thoughts of one subgroup in Barbados.

5.1 Interview 1 (M33)

(M33 is 33 years old and medium-skinned. He has a first degree and is a medical doctor.)

What are your views on shadeism?

Beyond the shadow of a doubt, it does exist... When I was working at a place called Printapak, the policy was that management and management material always had to be at least fair-skinned. This was actually said ... that they didn't like a particular person because he didn't fit and what they actually meant was that his skin was too dark. After that, I didn't stay much longer, because I realised that my advance in that company would have been limited.

How would you describe your skin shade?

Medium to dark. It doesn't affect me now, but it might have done had I not been a professional., where qualifications matter more than anything else.

Would you say that qualifications could make up for the advantages or disadvantages of skin shade?

Not necessarily. I think that if you are a professional it doesn't matter, but if you were a dark-skinned secretary you might not do as well as someone who was fairer skinned with the same qualifications.

To what extent do you think shadeism affects different people differently?

Generally speaking in the workforce, I think that white people and some black people would prefer to employ fairer skinned people, but if you get a self-made black man, he will generally be more open minded, but this is subject to correction.

The view that skin shade can affect job prospects is borne out by some of the other respondents' comments. However, when I examined the profile of the respondents, there was no obvious correlation between skin shade and type of job. The level of education seemed to play a much greater role, as the interviewee has suggested above.

Do you think this situation is still ongoing?
Without doubt it has historical roots. At school I had a religious teacher who always gave the white boys As or good marks, despite the fact that they hardly ever answered any questions. The black boys were marked more or less fairly, but often his favouritism depended on their skin shade.

Favouritism in a school setting has been mentioned by other respondents. This suggests that shadeism pervades the society to such an extent that it is both inculcated in the home and reinforced in schools.

Does this exist in other areas?
I've come across women who have said that they wouldn't go out with a particular person because he was 'too black' and they make no bones about saying this.

This suggests to me that the people who make these comments have internalised shadeism in the way described by Fanon, and have taken on board the negative associations of blackness. Their somatic norm is obviously the white European one.

How do you feel about people of different skin shades?
I can see through skin shade and see people for who and what they are. Just like anyone else I like attractive people, but skin shade in itself doesn't really matter to me.

This comment reflects those of most of the respondents, who said that skin shade was not important in choosing friends or partners.

Do you think the importance of skin shade has anything to do with the generation you're from?
I feel that there are probably more people from the older generations who have shadeism fixed in their heads, but at the same time people who I might consider forward-thinking feel as I do. There are people in the older generation who make comments about nice skin and nice hair, and essentially they are talking about the straightness of your hair and the blackness of your skin.

Is this based on a European ideal of beauty?

Yes. I think it's got historical roots. On the one hand you have the darker people who tended to be more African being labourers and having few prospects, while those who were white, fair or approaching white tended to have money in the family. Part of the reason why the views on shadeism may be changing may simply be that things are becoming a bit more evenly spread with regard to economics, but this is pure conjecture.

Although this interviewee sees shadeism as a generational phenomenon, this was not borne out by my analysis of the questionnaires. The people who said they were aware of or had experienced shadeism were of a variety of ages, as well as social and educational backgrounds. This does not suggest much change in the way shadeism is perceived and experienced.

Is there a difference between how skin shade is treated in a Barbadian context and in a UK context?

There's a big difference. In the UK with black people in a minority, shadeism doesn't really come into it – black people tend to regard themselves as being black or not.

There are some mixed race people who have a problem identifying with one group or the other – I have three cousins in London, two of whom have said that they will not date black women.

This bears out my earlier comments about the unifying political identity of 'black' in areas where non-white peoples are in the minority.

Are interracial relationships a big feature of the Barbadian scene?

Not particularly. There are short-term holiday relationships with the guys on the beach who are looking to make a quick dollar. I do know a few black Barbadian men who are married to white men, and fewer black women who are married to white men, and usually these white people are not Barbadian.

How do you think the issue of skin shade affects how people choose their partners?

By and large, men in particular will choose a woman who is fairer. I'm not sure why this is, whether it's one of these old things that fairer women are more attractive in some way.

Men seem to like women who have straighter hair, but a lot of financial and economic matters come into it. Given the choice of marrying a poor 'red-skin' woman or a well off dark woman, I think that is probably more important than shade. I think a woman is far more likely to choose a man of any shade, provided he is well off.

While analysis of the questionnaires does not indicate much difference in men and women's perceptions of attractiveness, the comments by many respondents bear out those of this interviewee. One can only surmise that in going for the lighter skinned women, black men may be reasserting their masculinity and conquering what was denied them during the days of slavery. Black women, on the other hand, are looking for economic stability.

If you had to choose to be two shades darker or two shades lighter, which would you choose and why?
To be very frank, I'd probably choose to be two shades lighter. I'd probably get by a little more easily in life. This is in contradiction to what I said on the questionnaire, but having had time to think about it, I think it might make life easier. It might mean I could get served more quickly in shops – I feel it would stand me in better stead.

This indicates some ambivalence about the issue of shade. Although this interviewee is a professional and as such, by his own reckoning, less affected by shadeism, he still feels that in terms of social acceptability and the small things which improve the quality of life, he would prefer to be of a lighter shade. This is a feeling echoed by many of the respondents, and one is tempted to believe that they can't all be wrong.

5.2 Interview 2 (F70)

(F70 is 33 years old and medium-skinned. She has a first degree and is a makeup artist.)

Have you ever experienced or observed shade discrimination?
The incident that comes to mind is the comparisons that were made between me and my sister who is perhaps two or three shades darker than I am.

When we went back to Barbados in our teens, people tended to call me the 'pretty one' and I know that my sister felt badly about it and I felt badly for her, and I realised that there was a real preoccupation with the shade of one's skin.

My grandfather, who would perhaps be called red, used to complain if I went out in the sun all day and looked burnt when next he saw me. The perception from a range of people from white to dark was that it was undesirable to have dark skin – to have a pretty medium colour was the thing.

This again brings up the question of a generational difference in the approach to shadeism. As I have stated above, the results of the questionnaire do not suggest that shadeism is any more or less prevalent among a particular age group. However, comments do seem to suggest a generational difference in the way people express their feelings about shade. Perhaps because it is seen as politically incorrect, younger people seem to be less open (or perhaps less decided) about their feelings on this issue.

What are the roots of this preoccupation with skin shade?
It has to come from slavery inasmuch that the darker slaves worked in the fields and the lighter slaves were given the house jobs and the slave women were encouraged to put forward their mulatto children for certain jobs, so it became associated with advancement.

Do you think this affects women more than men or is it pretty equal?

It definitely affects women more than men, because the perception of female beauty tends towards the white woman, as the ideal, as the model. So the closer a black woman is to looking white, the more beautiful she is usually considered, as evidenced in our beauty contests and jobs in industries that are perceived to be glamorous – the women tend to fit a light skinned profile.

How does shade affect choosing partners?

I think black men in Barbados don't tend to look to white women, maybe because they feel they would be unavailable to them, but they seem to favour slim, so called brown skin or fair skin women with long hair. I think that is the ideal – that is the sort of women that most men seem to look twice at. And from my conversations with male friends, it seems that the girls that they remember as attractive from their schooldays are always the ones who fit that bill. Women don't seem to have that problem. Women's choices seem to be based on a man's financial profile – what he does for a living is terribly important, and his height. His shade is a secondary consideration.

This comment bears out the feeling that women are more affected by shade discrimination than men are, in terms of the way they are perceived. However, when making their own choices, they do not let shade interfere with the important question of financial stability.

> *How does this affect job prospects?*
>
> I think it depends on the field, Certainly, in a clerical field, I think that fair skinned women tend to be chosen for secretarial and PR type jobs where they're going to be in the public eye. For a doctor or a lawyer it would be less important. In Barbados now you can see politicians in locks and twists – they don't seem to have to fit that standard, but anybody else does. A lot of Barbadian politicians have a law background and it is that that allows them to have their own individual style.

This response in some ways corroborates that of Interviewee 1 in that professional qualifications are perceived to mitigate any disadvantages conferred by skin shade. However, the notion that someone who is in the public eye who is not a professional (i.e. not a doctor, dentist or lawyer) is more acceptable if of a lighter hue again reinforces the idea of a white somatic norm in a largely dark-skinned society.

If you had to be two shades darker or two shades lighter, which would you choose and why?

I had tremendous difficulty with this question on the questionnaire, because there was a part of me that really wanted to select lighter, and I had to search my heart. I actually selected darker because I feel that my sister and my son are darker and if I were to go two shades lighter, there would be more of a gap, and it would be even more of an issue for other people, and maybe even for my son or my sister. And rather than make the differences between us more apparent I would want them to be less apparent.

Why were you considering choosing lighter?

Probably because I know that lighter skinned women tend to get more attention – there are more opportunities, more makeup choices for them. I don't consider that lighter equals more attractive (I don't subscribe to that at all), but I do recognise that lighter often equals more opportunity, more privilege.

This suggests a similar ambivalence to that shown by Interviewee 1.

Do you think shadeism will ever change?

It is as fundamental to the way that people think in the Caribbean – I think it's far too ingrained to change. And it's not only ingrained in the Caribbean, it's world-wide, so even if you leave the Caribbean to live somewhere else, you will find it manifesting itself in a different way – it's just one of those things that we are living with, and we subscribe to it without knowing it sometimes ourselves. The example that springs to mind is advertisements for skin toning or bleaching creams seen in women's magazines. The purpose is to lighten dark patches up to match the lighter patches, and I actually feel that given that we don't see advertisements for products that will darken your lighter patches, it suggests that to be lighter is to be more attractive. And a lot of black women, myself included, have bought creams for that very reason.

This again suggests that the view that lighter is better has been internalised by many sectors of society.

5.3 Interview 3 (F59)

(by email)

(F59 is 29 years old and medium-skinned. She has a first degree and is a student.)

Are you aware of shade discrimination in Barbados?

Yes, in the school that I attended there was definite shade discrimination. The white girls played indoors on the trampoline, the 'medium' girls or those who were black but could pass for white sat on the steps or played tennis. The black girls (those whose fathers were not politicians) played in the fields. It was a microcosm of slave society. Many of the lighter-skinned students tried to associate more with the whites than the blacks.

In what contexts does it tend to occur?

Shade discrimination occurred most often when it came to shopping in Bridgetown. First of all, most of the girls behind the counter were fair-skinned, which was perceived as better and more desirable. As a customer, I was often looked down upon for not being light enough. It was hard to get good service. It is interesting to note that in Barbados, which is populated mainly by Black people, Iman's cosmetic line did not take off, whereas Clinique is the strongest seller. I think that shadeism (and related matters) is something that is absorbed very early. I remember having a black doll with very curly hair and thinking she was very beautiful 'except for her hair'. I did not rest until it was completely straight. Then I tried to get it curly again. Sounds familiar?

This could also be due to the long standing presence of Fashion Fair and other black skincare brands, and the fact that Iman is relatively expensive, although other expensive products for white skins are purchased regularly). This interviewee also brings up the important question of hair, which can be a deciding factor in the way shade is perceived. Unfortunately I was not able to draw any conclusions on this based on my research.

Have you ever been affected positively or negatively by it?

I do not think I have any deep-seated scars from it. Sometimes it can be irritating. I am sometimes confused, however...I think 'if I were lighter I would be able to do such and such' but I also sometimes wish I were darker. I know that I do perceive myself as darker than I actually am.

The implication here is that it is a negative to be darker skinned.

To what extent do other factors (educational or financial, for example) affect the impact of the shade of one's skin?
A lighter-skinned woman with little education can generally go farther than a darker woman in the same circumstances

Does shade affect people's choice of partner?
Definitely. I myself am part of that cycle. My father married two very light-skinned women. I am married to a man a bit darker than myself. I think it is a phenomenon that has lodged itself in the Black subconscious.

To what extent does one's age affect one's perception or perpetuation of shadeism?
I think that older people are more inclined to be judgmental about shade of skin.

However, as this interview and others show, younger people are not exempt from these judgements either.

If you had to choose to be two shades darker or two shades lighter, which would you choose and why.

As I said above, I am sometimes confused about this. Increasingly, however, I am happy as I am.

6. Emails and newsgroups

Given the large number of Barbadians who live outside the island, popularly believed to be a greater number than the 266,000 who actually live there, I decided to try some newsgroup postings to see if anyone had any thoughts on the matter. This was disappointing in some respects, as the dialogue never really got going. However, it did lead to contacts with several former residents and nationals of the island, and their comments proved illuminating. Some of these are summarised below.

One response came from a Norwegian man married to a Barbadian:

'When Petal and I are walking around in Barbados, we sometimes get comments from black men "find yourself a black man" and things like that, while they like light skinned girls – not white, but light brown ones. … In Barbados, almost all black men that want to be someone have a woman that is lighter than him. Any man driving a fancy car has a lighter woman in the passenger seat.'

This suggests that dark-skinned black men are in need of a trophy (in the form of a lighter skinned partner) to validate their social and sexual marketability. Though some white men look for a 'trophy' partner, skin shade is not a factor, as the white man, by being white, is already validated as an individual.

A male Barbadian journalist living in New York states:

'Discrimination based on the colour of people's skin in Barbados, whether Black or white, has followed similar patterns in the United States. Every Black Barbadian, by Black I mean, people who are not what one would call 'light' or 'Brown' skin and who is over the age of 50 has experienced discrimination based on 'shades' of Blackness. The discrimination was mostly social, meaning that some Blacks of that generation wouldn't allow their daughters to date people who were 'too Black' or their sons to marry women who were 'too Black.' In addition, brown skin Blacks often didn't socialise with 'jet Black Blacks.'

In the area of employment, 'light-skin' Blacks were often favoured over 'dark-skin' Blacks. In addition, there were many working class Blacks who wouldn't work in the 1940s and 1950s as household help in the homes of Blacks simply because they couldn't bring themselves to work for a Black person. As if that wasn't bad enough, many dark-skinned Blacks, both male and female, deliberately sought out spouses of a lighter complexion because they didn't want to have children who 'were too Black.'

It is a trend that was widespread in the Caribbean, especially in Jamaica. Fortunately, that pattern of discrimination has all but disappeared. Its demise can be traced to positive Black self-awareness in the post-independence period and to the effects of the civil rights movement in the United States. (email, 3/8/98)'

This response shows some of the terms used to describe black people of varying shades and suggests that it pervaded society, particularly in the earlier part of the century. It provides a striking example of the internalisation of racism at work, with black people discriminating against other blacks. However the results of my research contradict the view that shadeism has 'all but disappeared'. Rather, it still appears to be a major feature of Barbadian society.

I followed up this email with some additional questions:

Would you wish to change your colour or shade?

'No. The reason is simple. I don't believe that colour or shades of it make a person. That may sound lofty but I have met so many damn fools, cheats and worthless people of every shade, colour and size that I am not impressed with white skin colour. I would admit however, to some degree of prejudice and that is I favour Black people, not at my expense but as a marker. In my previous e-mail, I pointed out that many people in their personal relationships in the Caribbean, opted for mates of a light shade. Perhaps it was because they believe that the closer one got to white people the better. There is an old saying "If you are white you are alright, if you are brown you can stick around but if you are black you must stand back." In addition many Bajans knew that if they had fair-skin children their chances of moving up in the country were much better. Many Barbadians in my time wouldn't date or marry anyone who was "blacker" than they were. A major reason was self-hatred. They didn't like who they were.'

Have you ever experienced discrimination because of your skin colour?

'Yes. When I left Combermere in 1958, I couldn't get a job at any of the major white firms because they didn't hire people who were "too Black," even for jobs as clerks. I went for interviews arranged by my father who was a light brown skin man with relatively straight hair. So some of the companies assumed that I looked like him and invited me in for an interview but when they saw me, they didn't even treat me with the courtesy of a follow-up response to tell me about the outcome of the interview. Anyone who is black of my generation in Barbados, Jamaica and most of the Caribbean experienced discrimination.'

The view that people were discriminated against on the job market because of their skin shade has entered into popular consciousness in Barbados, although it is rare to actually hear of an example of it happening. This example is thus particularly useful in bringing home the everyday effects of shadeism earlier in the century.

This is borne out by an email from a Barbadian man living in Norway:

A certain amount of favouritism does exist. I don't think you can say discrimination in the sense that no Black person, for example, would refuse to rent another a room due to colour differences. Generally lighter skinned people are assumed to come from a better family background etc. The type of favouritism seen in my opinion is mainly of a sexual nature and mainly among some men who generally prefer women of a lighter colour. It is not prevalent among women.

Shadeism as you call it is definitely a remnant of slavery.'
(10/8/98)

While the comments about the social acceptability of lighter skinned people are valid, I cannot agree with the view that shadeism is not prevalent among women. As my research shows, it is only women who said they would choose their friends based on skin shade.

It was timely that while I was looking for posts on the subject of shadeism, I came across one on 'The truth behind Queen's College and its students'. Queen's College is considered one of the best schools on the island, and therefore one of the breeding grounds for the intellectual and financial elite. The following post offers another twist on the subject of shadeism:

'Having lived in Barbados for twenty years, 1971-1991, and visited often, I don't think the problems can simply be reduced to 'race'. There is, however, a definite polarisation in terms of *class*. And, in that respect, you will find class discrimination as much among the black professional (upper, middle) classes, as you will among some of the plantation-descended whites. Unfortunately, because blacks make up so much of the population (> 90%) and because statistically, there are more poor among them, there is enormous overlap between race and class issues there. And, what commonly appears to be 'race discrimination' is, in reality, class discrimination. ... I warrant that most of the 'segregation' you see there, which appears to be racial-based, is in reality class based.... I think also, in a small society, geographical place - like Barbados, these sort of class based behaviours are bound to show up more.'

This highlights another issue which needs to be considered – that of class. As the posting states, and as Hoetink and others showed, race and class have tended to overlap to such an extent since the days of slavery that it is virtually impossible to separate them.

7. Conclusions and suggestions for further study

While it is difficult to make blanket statements on the basis of this limited study, several issues are clear. Shadeism is generally perceived to exist by and among all shades, ages and educational levels in Barbados. The interviews suggest that men are more likely to choose partners based on shade, while women look for economic stability. There is significant evidence of a feeling that lighter skin makes one's progress through society easier, but also a substantial group who is happy with being dark skinned and would not want to change that fact. Most people agree that it is a phenomenon inherited from slavery and which continues to affect Barbadian society. However, some people indicated that class factors are also an issue. In the 1960s Hoetink surmised that the segmentation of society by shade and race might disappear with the removal of the white elite from power. Thirty years later that hasn't happened. The white elite still holds economic power, and whiteness remains the somatic norm among a large segment of the population. However, it does appear that among some people a black Caribbean image has more acceptability. One can't help but feel that a desire to escape from the white norm lies at the back of it. Indeed, the tendency to categorise people according to shade has not lessened noticeably. I believe that if the belief in the beauty of blackness were deep or strong enough, there would be no need for these affirmations. It seems unlikely, therefore, as long as there continues to be a white power elite, that this norm will ever disappear.

This research has thrown up a number of areas which need to be examined further. Two areas in particular suggest themselves. First, how economic factors and education affect shadeism, and whether this is different among women and men. Second, to what extent one's perceived shade is altered by hair type, a factor which was mentioned by a few respondents. It would also be useful to look at images of black people in cultural products and, in the long term, to broaden the study to compare the perception of shade among Black American and Black Caribbean society, as both have emerged from the experience of slavery.

Bibliography

Bastide, R (1977) 'Color, Racism and Christianity' in Stone, J (ed) *Race, Ethnicity and Social Change* California: Duxbury

BBC (1991) *Redemption Song*: Series of seven programmes on the Caribbean presented by Stuart Hall

Beckles, H (1990) *A History of Barbados*. Cambridge: Cambridge University Press

Birbalsingh, F (1988) *Passion and Exile: Essays in Caribbean Literature* London: Hansib Publishing

Bruhn Jensen, K and Jankowski, N W A (1991) *Handbook of Qualitative Methodologies for Mass Communication Research* London: Routledge

Clifford, J and Marcus, J E (1986) *Writing Culture: the poetics and politics of ethnography* California: University of California Press

Fanon, F (1967/1991) *Black Skin, White Masks* London: Pluto Press

Gilroy, P (1987) *There Ain't No Black in the Union Jack* London: Routledge

Gilroy, P (1993) *The Black Atlantic: Modernity and Double Consciousness* London: Verso

Glazer, S (Ed) (1985) *Caribbean Ethnicity Revisited* New York: Gordon and Breach

Goldberg D T (1996) 'In/Visibility and Super/Vision: Fanon on Race, Veils and Discourses of Resistance' in Gordon, L R et al (Eds) *Fanon: A Critical Reader* Oxford: Blackwell Publishers

Gollop, A (date unknown) *Shades of Spades*

Griffiths, J (ed) (1984) *Caribbean Connections* London: Commission for Racial Equality

Hall, S (1991) 'Old and New Identities, Old and New Ethnicities' in King, A O (Ed) *Culture, Globalization and the World-System* London: Macmillan

Hammersley, M and Atkinson, P (1995) *Ethnography: Principles in Practice* (2nd ed) London: Routledge

Hawkins, I (1976) *The Changing Face of the Caribbean* Barbados: Cedar Press

Hoetink, H (1962, 1967) *Caribbean Race Relations: A Study of Two Variants.* New York: Oxford University Press

hooks, b (1992) *Black Looks: Race and Representation* Boston: South End Press

Hurley, S (1997) 'Shadeism: A People Divided?' (unpublished essay)

Knight, F W (1990) *The Caribbean: The Genesis of a Fragmented Nationalism* New York: Oxford University Press.

Lewis, G K (1983) *Main Currents in Caribbean Thought* Baltimore: John Hopkins University Press

Lowenthal, D (1972) *West Indian Societies* London: Oxford University Press

Mittelhozer, E (1960s) Kaywana Heritage

Morrison, T (1990) *The Bluest Eye* London: Picador

Oostindie, G (Ed) (1996) *Ethnicity in the Caribbean* London: Macmillan

Richardson, J and Lambert, J (1985) *The Sociology of Race* Lancashire: Causeway

Richmond, A H (1955*) The Colour Problem* Harmondsworth: Penguin

Rodney, W (1969) *The Groundings with my Brothers* London: Villiers Publications

Skellington, R (1996) *'Race' in Britain Today* (2nd ed) London: Sage

Thompson, P (1978) *The Voice of the Past: Oral History* Oxford: Oxford University Press

Van Dijk, T A (1987) *Communicating Racism: Mapping the Language of Prejudice* California: Sage

Wetherell, M and Potter, J (1992) *Mapping the Language of Racism* Hemel Hempstead: Harvester Wheatsheaf

Williams, E (1970) *From Columbus to Castro: The History of the Caribbean 1492-1969* London: Andre Deutsch

About the author

Sharon Hurley Hall holds MA degrees in Media and Cultural Studies, and in Teaching and Learning in Higher Education. She helped develop and teach the MA Journalism programme at Coventry University. Sharon has been a professional writer for more than 25 years, and is certified in content marketing and email marketing.

Printed in Great Britain
by Amazon

33393080R00049